THE BUSINESS ORACLE

SPHERICLES™

Your Intuitive Guide To

Enlightened Business Behavior

by
Joanne Black & Christine Roess

For information on other products, please contact:

SPHERICLES PUBLISHING INC.
212 East 48th Street
New York, NY 10017
(212)308-3283

To purchase more copies of Sphericles, please use the order form at the back of the book.

The authors welcome comments, thoughts and experiences that are a result of using Sphericles.

Printed in the United States of America

Art and book design by Self & Moon Design

ISBN-0-9643680-0-5

First Edition, 1994
Second Edition, 1995

*This book is lovingly dedicated to
Molly and Roxanna,
daughters in flesh and
sisters in spirit.*

When we function from the place of spacious awareness rather than from our analytic mind, we are often surprised to find solutions to problems without having "figured them out". It's as if out of the reservoir of our minds which contains everything we know and everything we are sensing at the moment, all that could be useful rises to the surface and presents itself for appropriate action... We often call this quality of mind "intuition"... Unlike our thinking mind, which arrives at solutions through a linear process of analysis which we can follow, the intuitive mind seems to leap to a solution. Perhaps the process is going on outside the range of our consciousness, perhaps we are delving into regions of the mind where thinking in the conventional sense is not necessary... As we learn to listen with a quiet mind, there is so much we hear. Inside ourselves we can begin to hear that "still small voice within" ...the voice of our intuitive heart.

How Can I Help?
Ram Dass and Paul Gorman

Reprinted by permission of Alfred A. Knopf, Inc.

Contents

Acknowledgments

The path that we have traveled from the inception and creation of this guidebook to its completion has been crowded with guides, ancient and new, without whose very real direction, Sphericles would not exist.

Our friendship and work together began in the early 80's with frequent sessions throwing the I Ching. We were eager for access to wisdom drawn from ancient philosophies that honor the intuitive.

Gratefully, other oracles began to become available. The Runes delighted us with their power to speak directly to our personal concerns. Later came Medicine Cards, Sacred Path Cards and The Power Deck, which we were using for the first time when the idea of creating an oracle for business came to us.

We also have grown deeply from the many hundreds of people throughout our business careers who have trained us, allowed us to practice on them and strengthened in us the rich teachings that we now share with you.

Although we aren't able to acknowledge everyone in this space, we must recognize a special few, whose trust and confidence in our often unorthodox stand for the unseen took courage and wisdom.

Our deepest appreciation to Harvey Herman, Cathie Liebl, Sandra Meyer, Russ Natoce, Don Pizzi, Jerry Trautschold, Jim Selman and Elizabeth Neeld.

Drawing on her deep sense of spirituality and prolific creative ability, Devi Jacobs helped us shape Sphericles in many ways, including suggesting we work with a numerologist. We want to express our love and gratitude for her generous contribution. We also warmly acknowledge Judith Halek, a gifted interpreter of the ancient art of Numerology, for ensuring that each teaching was paired with its most powerful number.

To Byron Callas, Rita Reneaux, George deKay, Beth Grossman, Chris Trinka and Laura Gabriel who share our belief in Sphericles and went above and beyond the call of duty to help us get it published, we want to express our deep appreciation.

For her generous spirit and strong technical support, we are sincerely grateful to MaryJane Findley. For her powerful editorial eye, we thank Judith Yellen. For their beautiful design and tireless cooperation, we thank Steve Self and Lisa Moon Self.

In the spiritual arena, the list is long. Still we could not fail to especially remember Guramayi Chidvilasananda and Ram Dass. Both of these masters are exquisite embodiments of compassion and wisdom, always sharing the highest teaching: That the true guru is within.

Finally, we both feel blessed to have parents who had the wisdom to teach us to trust ourselves.

Preface

A decade ago, Professor Daniel Isenberg of the Harvard Business School faculty studied the thinking processes of 12 corporate executives. His research revealed that most successful senior managers do not closely follow the classical rational model of decision making. In reaching this conclusion, Professor Isenberg joined other scholarly writers who recognize that in practice business executives rely significantly on intuition. (These writers include Chester Bernard, Henry Mintzberg, Paul Lawrence and John Kotter.)

I often wake up in surprise at that moment of consciousness when I realize that I am a practitioner of business management. I consult to corporations as well as teach the capstone course in business strategy. I am surprised because I had almost finished college as a studio art major before I took my first economics or business course. Then as now, I know I am an artist and that accessing the intuitive is central for me.

I was blessed to make the transition from art to business under the tutelage of Robert Coles, Erik Erikson, John Galbraith, Barrington Moore, Kenneth Andrews, George Lodge and Roland Christenson — gentle intellectual giants who brought artistry to their teaching and were unafraid to speak from the heart, the residence of the intuitive.

When the time came for me to go out in the world, I sought out companies like CBS, Polaroid and Paramount. I was hired as a financial manager at CBS.

To be black, female, and hired in finance in 1973, suggested to me that CBS was up to something more than business as usual.

The last question in the last interview was, "Why should we hire you over any one of your Harvard Business School classmates?" I spontaneously replied, "Because before I was an MBA, I was an artist. So in addition to my analytic intellect, you'll also get my creative instincts." I was hired on the spot.

During my tenure at CBS I worked with masters of finance, technology and corporate strategy like William Paley, Arthur Taylor, and David Sonnenfeld. To my surprise and pleasure, calling on the intuitive was a regular business practice for these mainstream executives, and the source of the creative energy and vision from which the organization's vitality was nourished.

It was a great opportunity to directly witness the role of the intuitive in guiding major business enterprises from senior management levels. This experience has taught me to never deny the power of my own inner wisdom and has enabled me to appreciate myself as an artist on the loose in the domain of business.

Sphericles arrives on the business landscape as an inspired tool for accessing the intuitive. It was derived from the intuitive by two women whose professional lives have been devoted to bringing "heart wisdom" to corporate vision and action.

Serving as a mirror, each Sphericle reading makes available the depth of wisdom that is a match for the desire for knowledge and the openness to guidance of the consulting seeker.

I would love to see Sphericles enter mainstream management literature. I believe it will support managers hampered by the inconsistency around how they are "supposed" to think and the thinking processes which they have found to be the most effective, and satisfying perhaps even blissful.

I've known Christine and Joanne for more than a decade. I have watched them commit to unpredictable, often outrageous outcomes. Based on the attendant miracles I've witnessed, I know that Sphericles is not a random toy. It is a gift from the heart to grace the world of work for all who will sincerely receive it.

Devorah Watkins Gilbert
Professor of Management
State University of New York
Stony Brook
1994

Introduction

Oracles have been used throughout history by shamans and seekers to access higher consciousness and benefit from their intuitive wisdom as they faced the challenges of life.

Sphericles combines the discipline of numerology with the ancient practice of using oracles to connect people to their inner wisdom for guidance in relating to their work lives.

Sphericles is based on an intuitively derived understanding that human beings are in the beginning stages of an evolutionary leap in relationship to work. Rather than relating to it as a survival-based activity forced upon us by the necessities of life, we are seeing the possibility of work as an expression of who we really are — as the contribution we are naturally designed to manifest. Our personality, talents, interests, even body-type are perfect for making this contribution, for doing the work that will be of greatest value to life.

Men and women are questioning the deeply ingrained orientation to competition and political games associated with business. We see the opportunity to recover the sense of community we long for in our work with others.

The best way we can tell if we are on the right track is by the presence or absence of joy. Joseph Campbell, one of the early teachers pointing the way to this new era, instructed us to "follow our bliss." This is a radical departure from the traditional view that work is hard and something we don't want to do.

In order to follow Campbell's intriguing advice, we must be able to tap into and trust our intuitive sphere. Until recently, we have mostly been taught to mistrust or ignore the whole domain of "feelings."

We're not very good at distinguishing the intuitive messages we receive, really continually, if we were awake to notice them. Even if we are doing work we love, we often get side-tracked by our concerns and conflicts and find ourselves operating out of old destructive habits.

Sphericles are offered as a guide to assist in accessing the powerful, life-enhancing and almost totally neglected source of inner direction for our professional lives. Sphericles do not promise to make work easy. Real work, like real play, is always a challenge that fully engages the players and requires the best of them.

Sphericles are designed as a vehicle to help you open up to what is true, responsible and satisfying for you in one of your primary activities of life — your work.

Sphericles work, not because there is magic in them, but because there is magic in you — always has been and always will be. Whenever you trust your intuition, true guidance shows up.

We all have the deepest wisdom for any problem as close to us as our breath just waiting for us to ask and... listen!

—— Consulting Sphericles ——

Sphericles are here to support you in gaining access to your intuitive wisdom to guide you in discovering your true path and authentic self-expression in your work.

Although Sphericles often give insight into the future, they are not a fortune-telling device. The most effective way to use Sphericles is to focus on what you want to have happen and ask what you need to learn or practice in order to get there. The Sphericle you choose will be your own higher wisdom speaking to you.

Sphericles give you an opportunity to intervene in those unwanted habitual responses that are more a reflection of how you have been conditioned than of who you truly are and can be. As a result, your work will be more and more creative, becoming an expression of your highest vision, your deepest desire.

Sphericles can be used individually, in partnership or in teams. There are One Sphericle readings and Three Sphericle readings for you to choose from. We also encourage you to design your own form for using them.

When To Use

Draw a Sphericle in the morning and use the reading as a centering ritual to focus your day. Use them spontaneously, such as before a major meeting or event, for guidance to support the best outcome. Sphericles are useful anytime you are confused, stuck or in need of inspiration.

How to Use

Sit quietly for a moment and contemplate the question or situation.

Clear your mind as much as possible and breathe easily as you put your hand into the Sphericles pouch.

Draw one or more Sphericles depending upon the kind of reading you are doing.

Read the number on the Sphericle and find the corresponding reading in the book for the insight and appropriate action to guide you in enlightened and effective business behavior.

—— Formulating Questions ——

Any issue that relates to your ability to bring pleasure and power to your work can be illuminated by Sphericles. For example, you can ask for guidance on how to handle a difficult co-worker, grow as a leader, expand your contribution and satisfaction at work, change jobs or open your own business. Simply say, "I am asking for guidance regarding... (and specify the problem or opportunity you have in mind.)"

Sphericles can be used by one person or a team of any number to provide guidance and enrich thinking and dialogue about constructive, enlightened responses to difficult situations or exciting opportunities.

Sphericles do not answer "yes" or "no" questions. They give you insight into how your way of relating and operating could further the best possible outcome for all concerned.

Based on these insights, the suggested actions will support you in operating in a way to produce the optimum result.

These actions are recommendations and, like everything in life, should pass the test of your own inner wisdom. Do not take any action that you believe would not be supportive. Remember, the point is always to have you more in touch with your own natural knowing.

You may also draw a Sphericle for someone else. They need not be with you. Just visualize the person and hold the issue in your mind when drawing the Sphericle.

—— Individual Readings ——

The following are suggestions for using Sphericles. You are encouraged to experiment with developing your own questions and format as well.

One Sphericle

This is the simplest use of Sphericles. Formulate the issue or outcome for which you want guidance and draw one Sphericle. The Sphericle you select will offer the wisdom you need to positively impact the situation that concerns you. It is your job to listen for the applicability, trusting that what you are hearing is neither random nor accidental. This can be particularly helpful under stressful conditions but is useful whenever you want insight regarding any work-related issue.

Three Sphericles

This reading allows you to discover the value of the situation for you and everyone involved and the development required to realize the desired outcome.

After clearly identifying the issue, draw three Sphericles, maintaining the order in which you drew them. Ask the corresponding Sphericle the following question:

First: What is this situation here to teach me/us?

Second: What do I/we need to develop or learn in order to realize the desired outcome?

Third: How do I/we enlist the support of others to achieve the goal?

— Sphericle Readings for Groups —

Sphericles are ideally suited for inspiring deeper relationship between two partners or co-workers or among larger teams. They may be used to bring forth greater trust, joy and high performance when people are already working well together, or for conflict resolution when they are not.

Using Sphericles can be a light-hearted and playful way to strengthen relationship among a new team or to increase the momentum of one that is already up and running.

Partners or Co-workers

Two people may enhance a working relationship or clear up a conflict by sitting down together, relaxing and breathing easily, then naming the issue for which they are seeking inner guidance.

One person draws a Sphericle and asks the other to find the corresponding teaching and read it aloud. Then the process is reversed with the second person drawing the Sphericle and the other reading the teaching.

If the Three Sphericle Reading is chosen, share the selection and readings of the Sphericles as desired.

After completing both readings, discuss the applicability to the specific situation and agree on what actions your combined inner wisdom has revealed.

Groups of Three or More

Teams can do a One Sphericle or Three Sphericle Reading and discuss the applicability to their situation.

When appropriate, the group reading can be done with each member of the team drawing their own Sphericle and placing it in a circle. Each member reads their Sphericle aloud as coaching for how to most benefit the team. This reading will help everyone understand the challenge for each person as it relates to the project at hand.

Again, creativity in using Sphericles is always welcome; and above all, enjoy yourself!

Interpretation

Having chosen a Sphericle and found its corresponding reading, take a deep relaxed breath and open up to the inner guidance that wants to speak to you now. Read to yourself, silently or aloud. If you are with someone, it can be helpful to ask them to read it to you.

As you go over the quotation, teaching and action, listen to your inner voice for what occurs to you regarding your issue, whether it makes sense at first or not. This is a communication from the intuitive sphere, and many of us are unfamiliar with how to tune into our less rational, less aggressive voice.

Sometimes the first reaction to an intuitive message is to discount it, believing that it is not the appropriate teaching in this situation. For now, put that reaction aside and listen to all three sections of the Sphericle trusting that there is a valuable message for you here.

For example, a young executive was feeling estranged and uncomfortable with her boss after years of a very satisfying working partnership. The Sphericle she chose was "Righteousness." She thought this couldn't pertain to her because she is not the "righteous type." However, as she listened to the reading she started blushing and laughing.

She saw that ever since her boss had changed the strategy of the company, she had been quietly critical of his choices. She secretly disapproved of the new direction and in subtle ways had been undermining the effort.

The next day, after more fully examining her righteousness, she called her boss on his out-of- town trip and told him what she had realized. She apologized for having been quick to criticize and for taking away her support. He was delighted and confessed that he had been upset and wondering how to handle the problem she was becoming. They discussed the new strategy and she asked all the questions she needed to ask to be fully engaged. Her enthusiasm and support returned and so did the satisfying working relationship.

Sometimes the reaction is delayed. For example, a successful executive of very high principles drew the Sphericle for "Integrity." He was surprised by this response to his issue, which involved a suit he felt morally justified in filing. He put aside his resistance and just let the insight be there, trusting that there was something valuable in it for him.

In a meeting with his lawyer the next day he saw that he was not fully communicating with his most important ally. In this way, he was not functioning consistent with his own integrity. The suit was concluded in his favor a few months later.

One of the greatest benefits of using Sphericles is the opportunity to expand your thinking. The readings suggest new ways to look at issues, and it is especially valuable to discuss them with another person. Often the discussion will provide important insights for others as well as the person asking for guidance. Even if you are doing a reading by yourself, it can be useful to call a friend or co-worker and get their viewpoint on the meaning of the reading.

Sometimes group readings create the opportunity for people to have a sensitive discussion they have wanted to have but didn't know how to initiate.

Remember, your inner wisdom is the true authority, so trust yourself, and always, enjoy!

S P H E R I C L E S

0

Integrity

This above all, to thine own self be true;
And it must follow as the night the day,
Thou canst not then be false to any man.

William Shakespeare

Teaching

Integrity is the ground zero Sphericle, the one without which all teachings are meaningless. Attracting it means you are serious about what you want to accomplish and there is some area where you need to strengthen your foundation.

Webster's first definition of integrity is "an unimpaired condition." We are impaired in any area where we are not being true to ourselves. Being honest about where we are not living in accordance with our own standards is a sign of maturity. Until we achieve sainthood, there is always some area where our integrity can be improved.

This is a time for uncompromising introspection so that you can see what truth wants to be revealed. This process will enhance the value you produce and the value you receive.

Action

Focus on a work situation you care about and find a way to bring more integrity to it. It may be time to make the recommendation you believe in but know will be hard-won, or you may need to communicate something you have been avoiding saying. If you're unsure about how to proceed, discuss it with a trusted colleague.

1

Purpose

This is the true joy in life,
the being used for a purpose recognized by yourself
as a mighty one; the being a force of nature
instead of a feverish selfish little clod ...
I am of the opinion that my life belongs to the whole
community and as long as I live it is my privilege to
do for it whatever I can.

George Bernard Shaw

Teaching

People who are happy at work are people who are clear about the purpose or value of their work. The purpose may be a humble one that supports people in meeting simple needs, but its value to people is genuine.

Most people long to have their work be of value to others. This yearning is neither unrealistic nor naive. It is a sign of an awake and committed human being.

This Sphericle suggests that the answer to your question lies in addressing the purpose or value of your work. Identifying the purpose clearly, appreciating the value it contributes and being able to fully articulate it, will provide direction and inspiration to you and the people you work with.

Action

When people ask you what business you are in, see if you can articulate it in an inspiring way. If you don't see value in what you do, look honestly at the need for a career adjustment that could bring a greater sense of purpose and value to your work.

2

Love

It is better to sit by the temple and beg alms
than do work you don't love...
Work is love made visible.

> *Kahlil Gibran*
> *The Prophet*

Teaching

You are blessed to have the sweet strength of the Love Sphericle come to you today.

This is great news! What you love to do is exactly what you're supposed to be doing! It is also what will generate the most value for you and others. That's the way life works.

Your truest self wants to have your work contribute fully to all of life. By picking this Sphericle you are letting yourself know that it's time to look closely at your work through the lens of love.

Action

Be honest about how much you love your work. If you don't love it completely, have a conversation with a creative friend about how you could more fully incorporate what you do love into your work.

3

Inspiration

It is like coming across a light
in thick darkness;
it is like receiving treasure in poverty.

Yuan-Wu

Teaching

This is the Sphericle that comes to release you from the part of your work that you experience as mundane or burdensome. Whenever you are working from an inspired state, there is pleasure. Even the challenging aspects of the project are rewarding.

You are being invited to see how you can shape your work life to make it more inspiring for yourself and others. This Sphericle is also a reminder of the power you have to be inspired, regardless of the circumstances. It isn't difficult. It's as natural as breathing. Inspire actually means to breathe in.

Start by expressing a sincere intention to be inspired. Then know that with practice, inspiration will come and your work will be imbued with energy, joy and velocity.

Action

Practice being inspired by "ordinary" acts of kindness and simple accomplishments. Also, look to see how you can design your current routine to make it more personally inspiring. For the long term, continue to direct your career toward work that you do with the most joy and the greatest ease.

Service

I do not know what your destiny will be,
but one thing I do know:
those among you who will be truly happy
will be those who have sought and found
how to serve.

Albert Schweitzer

Teaching

Today you have drawn a secret teaching about where the worldly and the sacred come together.

As business fully awakens to the joy and profitability of genuine service, the whole community will begin to blossom and thrive. People will experience that their work really counts. They will have a deep sense of respect and love for their organization and the value it creates for the society it serves.

Attracting this Sphericle is a strong indication that your heart is open and eager to deepen the experience of service in your work and to lead the way for others.

Action

Identify one area where you can enhance the service your work provides. In addition, find one immediate opportunity to be of service to someone at work. It doesn't have to be a dramatic or grand deed. Choose someone you don't often think of. Don't tell anyone that you did it.

5

Risk

Security is mostly a superstition.
It does not exist in nature...
Avoiding danger is no safer in the long run
than outright exposure.
Life is either a daring adventure or nothing.

Helen Keller

Teaching

The Risk Sphericle comes to coax you out onto the razor's edge of creativity. Sound frightening? How does staying locked in the same old dull routine sound?

Growth almost always requires opening up to the experience of genuine risk. The question you are asking yourself by picking this Sphericle is: Do I want to play a great game and go for my true vision, or do I want to be cautious, possibly bored and dissatisfied, kidding myself that I'm safe?

Every Accomplishment you're really proud of undoubtedly involved stepping into the unknown in some way. Trust yourself and go for your dreams.

Action

Identify an area of your work life where you are dissatisfied and suspect you are playing it safe. Think of one action you could take that would be outside of your comfort zone and take that action.

Connection

Despite the distances we have created...
Deep within us we feel a strong yearning
to leave the I-thought
and replace it with We-thought.
We are longing for harmony with ourselves...
harmony with the creation.
And that means inter-connectedness.

> *Rolf V. Osterberg*
> *The New Paradigm In Business*

Teaching

The degree of connection we feel with others is essential to our experience of pleasure at work.

We all have known people who we say are "on our wave length." When we have that connection, communication is natural and everything is right with the world.

This Sphericle encourages you to discover your ability to create connection wherever it is needed. Your success lies in facilitating this life-enhancing process with everyone you work with both inside and outside your company.

Action

Choose someone at work with whom you do not feel a natural connection. It may be that others have trouble connecting with this person too. Resist agreeing with others and make it your business to connect.

7

Stillness

Breathing in, I calm my body.
Breathing out, I smile.
Dwelling in the present moment
I know this is a perfect moment.

Thich Nhat Hanh

Teaching

Rarely do we consider being very still a powerful response to a situation, and yet it is perhaps the favorite strategy of those who have real mastery in life. Teachers in the art of being effective (for example in the martial arts) know that being quiet but fully alert will usually allow the situation to find its own resolution.

This Sphericle was guided to your hand by the wisest part of yourself who wants you to pause and become, not fixed or rigid, but one-pointed and silent like an owl in a tree on an utterly windless night.

Do not confuse stillness with passivity or denial. This teaching is asking you to bring a quality of presence that will allow everyone involved to be calmer and more able to choose life affirming behavior.

Action

Stop trying to figure out what to do, and commit yourself to becoming still. Whenever you find yourself anxious to leap into action, say to yourself "I'm trusting this one to work itself out."

Success

The joy, the triumph, the delight, the madness!
The boundless, the overflowing, bursting gladness,
The vaporous exultation not to be confined!
Ha Ha! The animations of delight
Which wraps me, like an atmosphere of light,
And bears me as a cloud is borne by its own wind.

Percy Bysshe Shelly

Prometheus Unbound

──────────────── **Teaching** ────────────────

Yes! Yes! Yes! You are about to experience success in some area of your work. Allow yourself to
experience the joy and satisfaction you have earned. Let
your body have the physical thrill. Let your voice express the extent of your appreciation. Include everyone who supported you.

The celebration of success with gratitude and generos-
ity breeds accomplishment in all aspects of your life. It
demonstrates to your higher self that you honor and put
to good use the flow of creativity we are all a part of.

Open your mind, body and spirit to the sweet sensa-
tions of success coming to and through you.

──────────────── **Action** ────────────────

Every day for one week notice, share and celebrate
everything that is a success for you — big and small,
personal and professional. It could be as simple as your
starting to exercise, or as major as getting the job you
want. Whatever it is, celebrate in some fashion. A
simple, full bodied shout of joy is a celebration.

9

Forgiveness

If we could read the secret history
of those we would like to punish,
we would find in each life
a sorrow and a suffering
enough to disarm all our hostility.

Henry Wadsworth Longfellow

Teaching

It is time to open your heart and release a grievance you have been holding against someone.

Forgiving is not a passive or weak act, but a powerful event calling for courage and wisdom. It is the courage to be more committed to strong relationships, joy and workability than to being right. It is the wisdom to accept that all people do stupid and unkind things and we all need forgiveness.

We often refuse to forgive someone who we feel has injured us until we are sure they have been punished. In reality, forgiveness frees us from the energy drain of holding a grudge.

Forgiveness is a gift you give to yourself.

Action

Think of one person you have been holding a grievance toward whom you would be willing to forgive today — and forgive them.

10

Ambition

Let each of you find where your chance for greatness lies.

Chariots of Fire

Teaching

We often think of ambition as a bad thing, as in "wild" or "blind" ambition. This Sphericle comes to you today to emphasize that the only ambition that is damaging is ambition without integrity or responsibility.

The most respected and loved leaders are those who are straightforward about their goals with a sincere commitment to achieving them with integrity.

The Ambition Sphericle is here to let you know that it's time to be more public (in an appropriate way) regarding the goals and accomplishments you are committed to achieving.

Action

The intention of this Sphericle is to allow you to share your ambitions more openly and with a wider group of people.

Choose a goal for yourself — one that excites you. Think of two people you haven't shared this goal with and tell them about it. Brainstorm with them ways they could support you in taking the next quantum leap.

⏤⏤⏤ 11 ⏤⏤⏤

Cooperation

We cannot live only for ourselves.
A thousand fibers connect us
with our fellow men;
and among those fibers,
as sympathetic threads,
our actions run as causes,
and they come back to us as effects.

Herman Melville

Teaching

The Latin root of cooperation is working together, meaning forces in action for mutual benefit. Research in almost all the human sciences indicate that cooperation is a superior form of relationship in nature and in organization.

This Sphericle acknowledges your appreciation of the joy and creativity available when people work together supportively and the struggle and pain when they do not.

It suggests that the time is right for you to use your higher wisdom to lead the way to a new level of cooperation. The example you set has an amazing impact on those with whom you work.

Action

Regarding the issue for which you are seeking guidance, find an area where you experience a lack of cooperation. Take the point of view that it's your responsibility to bring it to the situation.

12

Imagination

There are no mistakes and it's never boring
on the edge of the imagination,
which is only pure spirit out having a bit of fun.

> *Hugh Romney*
> *AKA Wavy Gravy*

------------------ **Teaching** ------------------

When you were a child, you were the ruler of an incredible universe. You could create anything, from being a banana to being the prince or princess of a distant galaxy.

The Imagination Sphericle is daring you to open up to a powerful fountain of possibility, accomplishment and joy. Imagination is made welcome when you let your intuitive mind run free and your dreams flow.

Let go of your limiting beliefs with regard to the work issue at hand. To be truly imaginative requires a willingness to not know and a boldness when ready answers are insufficient to handle the challenges.

This Sphericle is counseling you to rely on your imaginative power in this situation. Throw your analytical mind to the wind and entertain fantasies your "sensible self" would never allow you to think.

------------------ **Action** ------------------

Pick a challenge or opportunity in your work and set aside time to capture your "beyond your wildest imagination" ideas, preferably with one of your more free thinking colleagues or friends.

— 13 —

Strategy

God is in the details.

Albert Einstein

Teaching

This Sphericle refers to the art and science of achieving your vision. Drawing it indicates you are, indeed, on the right track. It is now time to address the ways that you are going to bring it into reality.

This is no less a creative endeavor than crystallizing your vision. Identifying the avenues that can transform vision into reality is often the most challenging aspect of creation. Confronting this part of the process separates dreamers from leaders.

This Sphericle is telling you to act. Your vision is worthy. You are ready to discover the pathways to success. Don't give up.

Action

Choose one of your most important objectives and devise a strategy for achieving it. Share this work with a colleague whom you trust to be your coach and brainstorm further ideas. Continue this process until you have strategies for all the major objectives.

14

Trust

*It takes great learning
to understand that all things,
events, encounters and circumstances
are helpful.*

The Course in Miracles

Teaching

This is the Sphericle that marries wisdom and strength. It comes to you today to take your hand and give you courage to radically trust where until now you haven't been able or willing to let go.

Anyone can bring trust to a situation where all parties have demonstrated they are trustworthy. It takes courage to bring trust in order to shift an atmosphere of discord or suspicion to one of mutual support and teamwork. This is exactly what your own deep wisdom is asking of you now.

Remember to trust your own process. Whatever happens in this situation, know that it is leading you to expanded opportunities for love and growth.

Action

Find a project or a relationship where you wish there were more trust present, and commit yourself to bringing it.

Interpret the circumstances of this questionable situation through the lens of the Course in Miracles passage quoted above.

Team

Individual learning, no matter how wonderful it is
or how great it makes us feel,
is fundamentally irrelevant to organizations,
because virtually all important decisions
occur in groups.
The learning unit of organizations are "teams"
groups of people who need one another to act.

Peter Senge

─────────── **Teaching** ───────────

Any accomplishment that we can realize on our own is usually trivial. No matter how brilliant the idea, a team is required to make it happen. Work is an act of co-creation.

What blocks powerful teamwork is the concern for individual control, credit or blame. Ongoing struggle and ineffectiveness in any project is a signal that those involved are more committed to expressing their individuality than they are to the project.

The outcome you seek now requires your leadership. Strengthening the team will enable the project you care about to come to fruition.

─────────── **Action** ───────────

Identify three team members relevant to your project and enlist their commitment to a new level of team performance. The most essential ingredient in gaining their support will be some genuine shift in your point of view regarding who can participate and in what way.

16

Resignation

The most notable characteristic of
the managers I interviewed
was their mannerly lack of intensity.
Nothing seemed to matter very much.

Diane Margolis

The Managers:
Corporate Life in America

Teaching

Y̲ou draw this Sphericle to you as a "wake up call." It is a call to confront an aspect of your work life where you are not happy but feel resigned to putting up with the situation.

Resignation is one of the most effective conditions for keeping us stuck in life. It's the listless, "oh what's the use, there's nothing I can do about it anyway," point of view. We all have made decisions about what is possible (or not possible). Because of their transparent nature, we don't see these decisions as our interpretation. We see them as "the facts."

What is required is the recognition that you have become resigned. Once recognized, your inner guidance is absolutely able to lead you out of this debilitating state.

Action

I̲dentify an area where you have become resigned. It might be a difficult relationship or a burdensome job responsibility. Pick a person whom you can trust to stand in firm opposition to your negative interpretation and ask them to help you see with new eyes.

SPHERICLE

17

Abundance

To see the World in a Grain of Sand
And a Heaven in a Wild flower
Hold Infinity in the palm of your hand,
And Eternity in an hour.

William Blake

Teaching

What a delicious reminder of this rich experience we call life! Abundance as a quality to work from provides an enormously blissful and generative flow.

We human beings are prone to see life through the eyes of scarcity. This vision of life makes money, success, time, even love seem to be scarce.

You have chosen this Sphericle today because your wisdom self wants you to see through the eyes of abundance. You are being asked to trust that the universe is delighted to shower all its gifts on you if you will genuinely open to it.

Action

Think of something you consider to be scarce in your work life. For one day, adopt the point of view that it isn't scarce. Take three actions consistent with the eyes of abundance.

18

Breakdown

Between 1971 and 1975
Fred Smith (founder of Federal Express)
fell $30 million in debt,
was indicted for defrauding a bank,
got sued by his own family,
and saw his investors replace him
as commander of his company
then got it back again.

Nayak and Ketteringham
Breakthroughs!

Teaching

S uccess is primarily determined by the ability to function in the face of intimidating breakdowns. In fact, virtually all major breakthroughs are preceded by breakdowns! If you can't tolerate breakdowns, you won't be able to commit to big projects.

Drawing this Sphericle alerts you to a current or impending breakdown in an area of your work that needs your creative and nurturing attention.

The Breakdown Sphericle suggests that you view road-blocks as gifts in disguise. Avoid the temptation to collapse into blaming yourself or others. Successful people not only manage themselves in the face of breakdowns, but also support others in letting go of blame and staying in constructive action. The reward for this response will be amazing effectiveness and joy!

Action

F ind someone who shares your commitment and explore the following: What is this breakdown teaching you? What new directions could you take if you let your thinking expand? What support is needed by the people involved to keep their energy high?

19

Leadership

True leaders inspire people to do great things,
and when the work is done,
their people proudly say,
"We did this ourselves."

Lao-Tzu
Tao Te Ching

Teaching

This teaching is a reminder of the qualities of real leadership, versus the grandiose fantasies sometimes associated with leadership.

The qualities of real leadership include:

- Wisdom and commitment to generate a compelling vision.
- Passion and creativity to inspire others to act.
- Compassion and trust to create a safe environment where people can stretch and make mistakes.
- Respect and appreciation for others.

Drawing this Sphericle is saying that you have the ability and the opportunity to lead. It is time for you to strengthen your natural leadership qualities. Open and listen to the part of you that is calm, wise and loving. You will be delighted at what begins to happen.

Action

Review the qualities of leadership in the teaching. Choose those that will make the most difference in the project. Practice expressing these qualities. Ask someone in a position to observe you in action to give you feedback.

20

Listening

But each ear is listening to its hearing,
so none hear.

W. H. Auden

Teaching

If there were one solution to the dissatisfaction and frustration people experience at work, it would simply be having everyone really listen to each other. The problem is it always seems to be the other person who isn't listening.

The silence required for powerful listening isn't so much keeping our outer voice quiet; it is keeping our inner voice quiet. The inner voice is the one that's already rehearsing what we're going to say next or refuting what's been said before we've thought about it or even heard it completely.

Very few people seriously work on developing their ability to listen. This Sphericle comes to you now to ask if you are willing to listen with a power, a respect and a stillness that you've never had before.

Action

Who is it you resist listening to? Ask yourself honestly what it is that you fear would happen if you really listened to that person. Commit yourself to listen to them with respect for three consecutive conversations. Let them know you really are listening by periodically paraphrasing what they are saying.

S P H E R I C L E

21

Sales

Sell: 1. To give up in violation of duty, trust, loyalty: Betray.

Webster's Ninth Collegiate Dictionary

Teaching

This Sphericle comes to you now to support you in profitably concluding an important transaction. Webster's strongly negative definition of "sell," as in "sell-out," reveals why many of us are uncomfortable with the sales conversation. We have seen how easy it can be to let the integrity slip, just a little, in the form of exaggeration or undue pressure.

Powerful selling today is characterized by a commitment to open and honest communication. Great salespeople know that maintaining a relationship of respect and trust with the customer is the primary concern.

Whether it is a contract, promotion or recommendation they want others to embrace, masterful sales people follow three tenets:

- **Make sure you ask directly** for what you want.
- **Listen attentively** and with a commitment to hearing your customer's concerns.
- **Always validate the customer's choice** whether or not you made the sale.

Action

Think of something at work that you would really like to have happen. Think of it as a sales transaction, even if it doesn't seem to fit the usual definition of sales. Now, go make a clear request to the person involved. Pay special attention to your own clarity in communicating the benefits and costs. Listen carefully and validate their choice.

Power

What gives power its charge,
positive or negative,
is the quality of relationships.
Those who relate through coercion... create
negative energy.
Those who are open to others and see others
in their fullest create positive energy.
Love in organizations, then, is the most
potent source of power we have available.

Margaret Wheatley
Leadership And The New Science

Teaching

This Sphericle portends a significant leap in your development. It is the profound learning of becoming responsible for your power.

Many people are so determined to avoid the negative use of power, they refuse to let their power out at all. They stay in the background lamenting the abuse of power by others.

In drawing this Sphericle your higher wisdom is telling you that your power to generate a life-enhancing vision is expanding. You are being asked to remember that the highest power is that which creates love in all its forms.

Commit yourself to lead with love and compassion and then go for what you really want to contribute in life. It's time.

Action

With regard to the most exciting goal you have, take a stand for yourself as powerful and loving and make at least one bold request. Be sure others are also empowered by your action.

23

Possibility

*The best way to predict the future
is to create it.*

Peter Drucker

Teaching

This teaching is about stepping outside of your present way of thinking and seeing a new future for your work. It is time to be open to a shift in what you see is possible, not because you have proof it will happen but because you are willing to be responsible for creating it.

Innovation comes from people who are willing to go beyond accepted beliefs. You are ready to see what no one has seen before in some area of your work.

This Sphericle has come to you to encourage you to declare your vision and lead those around you in making it happen.

Action

Identify the area of your work where you know in your heart that something new is waiting to be created. Then have a conversation to explore the possibilities with a trusted colleague or friend. See what commitments you can make to add momentum to bringing it into existence.

24

Investment

You only get out of something as much as you put into it.

Everybody

Teaching

This Sphericle is here to announce that opportunity is knocking at your door! There is a perfect place in your life right now to invest your resources, whether it is time, money or quality attention.

Be alert for opportunities outside the areas where success comes easily to you. Pay particular attention to anything that excites you and holds promise for the future.

Choosing the Investment Sphericle suggests that there is an area of your life that you want to start nurturing and developing. Listen to your higher wisdom, even if the opportunity requires resources you don't have at the moment. With your commitment to invest, what you need will come to you.

Action

The first step is to tell the truth about an area in your work life that interests you. See what investment is needed: time, money or creative energy and make the commitment to make that investment.

25

Righteousness

There is nothing to win or lose in group work.
Making a point does not shed light
on what is happening.
Wanting to be right blinds people.

Tao of Leadership

Teaching

The challenge here is to deal with the need to be right, even when it results in the loss of satisfaction, affinity and effectiveness. The Righteousness Sphericle is the close-to-the-bone teaching that no human being can hear too often.

It is the reminder to look and see where you are being right about your point of view and how it's costing more than it's worth.

As you learn the power of this Sphericle, you will be pleased to attract it and to share its lessons. A profound gain in confidence comes from tolerating the momentary ego-pinch of letting go of a tightly held opinion.

Real freedom lies in being able to open to another point of view.

Action

Review the trouble spots in your work life and fearlessly identify where you are being right in a way that isn't working.

26

Competition

The trouble with being in the rat race is that even if you win, you're still a rat.

Lily Tomlin

Teaching

This Sphericle is telling you that the time has come to focus on the way you achieve your goals. Finding the relationships where you are behaving competitively, perhaps without being aware of it, is the first powerful step.

Shifting from a competitive way of operating to one of mutual support and collaboration will bring you a level of success that has eluded you as well as greater satisfaction and pleasure in your work.

It may be that a person or organization that you consider to be a competitive threat could offer a strategic alliance that would benefit everyone.

Action

Identify one person with whom you feel competitive in your work. Arrange a meeting with that person, perhaps over lunch, with the goal of finding some way you can cooperate that will benefit both of you.

27

Acknowledgment

Really great people have a curious feeling
that the greatness is not in them,
but through them.
And they see something divine
in every other person.

John Ruskin

Teaching

I f you have chosen the Acknowledgment Sphericle, you are ready to have your environment at work be more loving and self-affirming. You are remembering that human beings blossom under the sunshine of having their value, great or small, noticed and appreciated.

Relationships flourish and morale problems are unheard of in organizations where acknowledgment is commonplace. There is no conversation you can initiate that empowers teamwork and effective performance more.

If your organization isn't full of acknowledgment, your inner self is asking you to take the lead in developing this nurturing and creative atmosphere. Any acknowledgment that is a genuine expression of appreciation will create affinity and pleasure.

Action

T ake every opportunity to acknowledge people both at home and at work. In addition to the major accomplishments, be alert to the everyday contributions other people make, like making sure the plants are watered or lightening up a drab day with a smile or a joke.

28

Focus

It takes a person who is wide awake
to make their dreams come true.

Roger Babson

Teaching

Many people know a lot about doing things right. The challenge here is knowing the right things to do. It is time to stop having new ideas or worrying about doing things right. It is time to focus.

If you are feeling pulled in many directions because there is too much to do, find ways to delegate some of the doing so that you can focus your thinking and energy on the essential.

This Sphericle is here to alert you that effort is being wasted on activities that are not central to the goal. It is your challenge to identify what is important and maintain the focus for yourself and those with whom you work.

Action

Examine where you are feeling scattered at work and identify the things you are doing that are not essential to your goal. Take at least one action today that will redirect the energy to your primary commitment.

29

Growth

The important thing is this:
To be able at any moment to
sacrifice what we are
for what we could become.

Charles Dubois

Teaching

Get ready for a leap in your development! Drawing this Sphericle lets you know that you are in for an exciting time that will lead to greater success and happiness for you.

The growth referred to here considers all aspects of your being to ensure that you are in balance. Remember, growth in business at the expense of your body, spirit, relationships with family and friends is not growth but, in fact, imbalance.

Don't resist the challenges that always come with growth. You are ready. This growth will support the continuous development of health and vitality in your life and the lives of those around you.

Action

Choose a task or project in your work life that, if acted on, would genuinely support your growth. This is likely to threaten some familiar habit, because that is where the greatest growth occurs. Think of an action you can take to start the process and begin.

30

Play

Angels can fly because they take themselves lightly.

G.K. Chesterton

Teaching

What's the difference whether work is experienced as work or play? Bringing the spirit of play to work is a sign of mastery. Struggling to get the job done is probably better than not getting it done at all; but don't be surprised if people aren't excited about working on the next project.

Many people have an unrecognized rule that they shouldn't get paid for having fun. The Play Sphericle begs, pleads, is down on its round knees weepin' just to convince you to risk looking foolish and even waste time in some real frolic.

You may be amazed at what gets accomplished when people are delighted and share good feelings. You'll want to waste this kind of time every day!

Action

Toy with the idea of how you can turn your work into play. How could you do that, in your specific case? Come on, really play with it.

31

Fired

*Dwell as near as possible
to the channel
in which your life flows.*

Henry David Thoreau

80

Teaching

It's time to fire yourself from some job or responsibility that is no longer satisfying. Your inner wisdom is telling you to act before someone else's outer wisdom makes the decision for you.

This Sphericle is pointing to an aspect of your work that you have outgrown but have been unwilling or unable to relinquish. It doesn't necessarily mean that you need to quit your job, although in some cases it may. Only you know what dead branch should be cut away to strengthen the whole tree and create some room for new growth.

Whether it's a responsibility you need to delegate to someone or actually leaving your job, take the leap. Your intuition is telling you it will be one of the smartest things you have ever done. Now is the time!

Action

Acknowledge where it would be growth producing for you to let go of one or more of your responsibilities. Discover the power of telling yourself "I'm fired" in this area.

32

Profit

Many men go fishing all of their lives without knowing that it is not fish they are after.

Henry David Thoreau

Teaching

This Sphericle asks you to notice the profit that is accruing through your action at work. It is profit that you have earned. However, it may not take the form you expect.

The dictionary defines profit as "valuable return; gain," not money. It is time to expand your definition of profit to include all the value you receive from your work. The value might be the opportunity to work with someone you admire or the discovery of a new talent you didn't know you had.

This Sphericle indicates profit is at hand beyond short term monetary gain. The value you receive is aligned with your true ethical standards and will contribute to your physical and emotional health.

Action

Spend today noticing where you receive profit in your life. Be especially alert for value in personal relationships and the experience of satisfaction and fulfillment.

The more you see profit in its many forms the more it will come to you.

33

Decision

Man is born to live and not to prepare to live.

Boris Pasternak

Teaching

This Sphericle comes to you now to suggest there is a decision to be made about something related to your work. You have done all the investigation that can be done. Those factors that are still unknown will become evident after the decision is made and action taken.

Even if the decision you make turns out not to be completely right, it will reveal important information that will guide you to the right path. To wait on this decision can only weaken your position. The time to make the decision is now.

Trust yourself. Do not hesitate any longer.

Action

Identify three decisions you are facing in your work. Select the most important and make the decision.

Joanne Black

J oanne Black was the first woman to serve as a vice president of marketing at American Express Co. Later, she was senior vice president of marketing at MasterCard International and Showtime Networks, Inc. Initiating campaigns that won nearly every industry award, she is recognized by her peers as one of the leading-edge thinkers in American business. She has been featured on television, in magazines and on radio as a pioneer and role model for women in business.

Throughout her career, Joanne has been a student of spiritual philosophy and an advocate for the value of intuition in business. As a partner in Business Dynamics, she often consults with clients on developing their intuitive wisdom at work.

She has served on the Board of Directors of the Association of National Advertisers and the Advertising Club of NY. She is a graduate of the Harvard Business School PMD program and is presently on the Marketing Advisory Board for the Graduate Program at Fordham University.

Christine Roess

C hristine Roess is founder of SDI Communica-
tions, a management consulting firm committed
to the transformation of business through conscious
communication. SDI's clients include AT&T and Mobil
Oil Corporation.

Christine graduated from the University of Michigan
and has been a student of eastern spiritual traditions
and new age metaphysical teachings for over twenty
years.

In 1984, she founded a women's organization in New
York City devoted to the development of leadership
from the feminine intuitive sphere. She is a member of
the Board of Directors of New York Youth At Risk
and a founding member of the Women's Economic
Circle.